SUMMARY

ALEXANDER HAMILTON

BY RON CHERNOW

BOOK JUNKIE

Alexander Hamilton

By Ron Chernow

Summary by Book Junkie

© Copyright 2016 by Book Junkie - All rights reserved

No part of this book may be reproduced in any written, electronic, recording, or photocopying without written permission of the publisher or author. The exception would be in the case of brief quotations embodied in the critical articles or reviews and pages where permission is specifically granted by the publisher or author.

Although every precaution has been taken to verify the accuracy of the information contained herein, the author and publisher assume no responsibility for any errors or omissions. No liability is assumed for damages that may result from the use of information contained within.

No responsibility or liability is assumed by the Publisher for any injury, damage or financial loss sustained to persons or property from the use of this information, personal or otherwise, either directly or indirectly. While every effort has been made to ensure reliability and accuracy of the information within, all liability, negligence or otherwise, from any use, misuse or abuse of the operation of any methods, strategies, instructions or ideas contained in the material herein, is the sole responsibility of the reader.

Table of Contents

Getting Started 2
What Type Of Book Is This? 2
Information on the Author 3

Summary 3
Observations by Alexander Hamilton 3
Prologue: The Oldest Revolutionary War Widow 3
Chapter One: The Castaways 4
Chapter Two: Hurricane 5
Chapter Three: The Collegian 6
Chapter Four: The Pen And The Sword 7
Chapter Five: The Little Lion 8
Chapter Six: A Frenzy of Valor 8
Chapter Seven: The Lovesick Colonel 9
Chapter Eight: Glory 10
Chapter Nine: Raging Billows 11
Chapter Ten: A Grave, Silent, Strange Sort Of Animal 11
Chapter Eleven: Ghosts 12
Chapter Twelve: August And Respectable Assembly 12
Chapter Thirteen: Publius 13
Chapter Fourteen: Putting The Machine In Motion 14
Chapter Fifteen: Villainous Business 14
Chapter Sixteen: Doctor Pangloss 15
Chapter Seventeen: The First Town in America 15
Chapter Eighteen: Of Avarice and Enterprise 16
Chapter Nineteen: City of the Future 16
Chapter Twenty: Corrupt Squadrons 17
Chapter Twenty-One: Exposure 18
Chapter Twenty-Two: Stabbed in the Dark 18
Chapter Twenty-Three: Citizen Genet 18
Chapter Twenty-Four: A Disagreeable Trade 19
Chapter Twenty-Five: Seas Of Blood 19
Chapter Twenty-Six: The Wicked Insurgents Of The West 20
Chapter Twenty-Seven: Sugar Plums and Toys 20
Chapter Twenty-Eight: Spare Cassius 21
Chapter Twenty-Nine: The Man In The Glass Bubble 21
Chapter Thirty: Flying Too Near The Sun 22
Chapter Thirty-One: An Instrument Of Hell 22
Chapter Thirty-Two: Reign of Witches 23
Chapter Thirty-Three: Works Godly And Ungodly 23
Chapter Thirty-Four: In An Evil Hour 24
Chapter Thirty-Five: Gusts of Passion 24

Chapter Thirty-Six: In A Very Belligerent Humor..25
Chapter Thirty-Seven: Deadlock..25
Chapter Thirty-Eight: A World Full Of Folly..25
Chapter Thirty-Nine: Pamphlet Wars..26
Chapter Forty: The Price Of Truth..26
Chapter Forty-One: A Despicable Opinion..27
Chapter Forty-Two: Fatal Errand..27
Chapter Forty-Three: The Melting Scene..27
Epilogue: Eliza..28

Criticism 28
Biographies 28
Alexander Hamilton September 11, 1755 - January 31, 1795..28
Eliza Hamilton August 9, 1757 - November 9, 1854..29
George Washington February 22, 1732 - February 11, 1731..30
John Adams October 30, 1735 - July 4, 1826..30
Aaron Burr February 6, 1756 - September 14, 1836..31
Thomas Jefferson April 13, 1743 - July 4, 1826..32

Getting Started

What Type Of Book Is This?

This is a historical non-fiction book, that draws from many primary and secondary sources to describe the events of Hamilton's life and the events of history. In particular, Chernow cites the large collection of Hamilton's papers that was published in the last few decades, and that has served as the basis for the biography he wrote.

As with any non-fiction book, it is tempting to take it at face value. However, how facts are presented can sometimes put a different spin on them. Chernow is obviously sympathetic to Hamilton, which is important to keep in mind when reading the book. Several criticisms also mention that Chernow is better at understanding the psychological motivations of the people involved than the historical context in which they acted.

Information on the Author

Ron Chernow is an author, journalist, and historian who has written a number of biographies and nonfiction historical books. He has written series covering the lives of JP Morgan, John Rockefeller, and the Warburg family. He has also written several best-selling biographies of George Washington, and Ulysses S Grant, many of which have won a range of awards, including National Book Critics' Circle Award, and a prize for excellence in economic writing.

Chernow is a graduate of both Yale and Cambridge University. He served for a short while as director of finance studies for the Twentieth Century Fund, and he continues to contribute articles to the New York Times, and Wall Street Journal.

Summary

Observations by Alexander Hamilton

These are a collection of four quotes from Hamilton's letters and essays. They generally seem to express facts as they are, rather than twist them to please a particular viewpoint. Several also seem to express a frustration that opinions, rather than reality, are often the determining factor when decisions are made. They are also very eloquent quotes.

Prologue: The Oldest Revolutionary War Widow

The book begins with Hamilton's widow, Elizabeth Schuyler Hamilton, waiting quietly in her house in Washington, D.C. to join her husband, who she refers to as, 'her Hamilton.' She was a tireless advocate for her husband, commissioning a multi-volume biography of Hamilton that would eventually be completed by her son after her death.

Alexander Hamilton remains a controversial figure, lauded by some as a defining figure in US history, and decried by others as a corrupter of its essential nature. He was the country's first Secretary of the Treasury, and it was under his guidance that the first national bank of the United States was founded, and he laid down the foundation for concepts such as a funded debt, tax framework, and many other aspects of the nascent country's financial infrastructure. In his 41 years he was, as the book lists, 'clerk, college student, youthful poet, essayist, artillery captain, wartime adjutant to [George] Washington, battlefield hero, congressman, abolitionist, Bank of New York founder, state assemblyman, member of the Constitutional Convention and New York Ratifying Convention, orator, lawyer, polemicist, educator, patron saint of *New York Evening Post*, foreign policy-theorist, and major general in the army.'

He, along with James Madison, was one of the primary architects of the US Constitution. He was also one of the authors of, and a guiding force in, the *Federalist*, which remains an eloquent justification for a strong central government.

Hamilton was, in addition to all the rest, a habitual writer. His letters and journals offer insight into the life of the time, as well as the lives of the Founding Fathers and the people who ran the early US Government. A comprehensive collection of his writings were published in 27 volumes, and Chernow has drawn heavily on these works in writing the biography. He also used records from a number of places, including England and Hamilton's birthplace in the Caribbean to develop a comprehensive picture of Hamilton's life.

Chernow says it is a good time to examine Hamilton's life. The US has moved definitively away from its agrarian roots to become an economic power, with a central bank, powerful stock markets, and heavy industry, all of which are based on the vision Alexander Hamilton had of the US's future and the system he helped create.

Chapter One: The Castaways

Alexander Hamilton's father, James Hamilton, was the fourth son of the Laird of Grange, a scottish noble. James was considered feckless but amiable. His family was wealthy, and his brother, John, tried to shepherd James into a good profession. Eventually he would be shipped off as the business's agent on St. Kitts. There, he was constantly being bailed out by his wealthier brother and their industrial friends. James likely did did not realize how his brother was helping him, and he did his best to conceal his financial problems. It is likely that his fortune was in ruins before he even met Hamilton's mother, Rachel

Rachel had already had an interesting life. She had been given in marriage to Johann Lavien, who would turn out to be a rascal and failed conman. They ended up living apart, something that humiliated Lavien. Due to a law on Nevis, where they lived, he was able to have Rachel put in jail, a horrifying prospect in the 18th century. Once she is released, she leaves the island, leaving behind her husband and a son. She was leaving not just a broken marriage, but accusations of infidelity behind.

James and Rachel met on St Kitts, and though they never married, they lived together as a couple. Rachel gave birth to two sons: James Jr. and Alexander Hamilton.

Which year, precisely, Hamilton was born remains something of a mystery. He and his family measured his age from the year 1757, though some evidence argues for moving that date back to 1755. Rachel inherited a townhouse from her father in the city of Charlestown, the capital of Nevis, and Hamilton likely grew up there. Kept from school by his illegitimate birth, he received tutoring, both from his mother and from others. It is from his mother that he most likely learned French, a language he would remain comfortable with for the whole of his life.

Even whites who were not wealthy owned at least a few slaves, and so it is very likely that Hamilton grew up with several slaves. Violence was commonplace. The slaves were treated, of course, terribly. They would be run down the road, naked, and flogged occasionally to keep them moving. Duels were also fought on the island, offering gory tales of honor and death to amuse the young Hamilton.

James would leave his family, and Rachel would be forced to work to support them until her death of a fever. Thier stepfather Lavien would return one final time, demanding Rachel's property for their son Peter. Some of Rachel's things were sold off to pay her debts, though one of the Lyttons was kind enough to buy the books back for Alexander. In any case, the court awarded all of Rachel's property to Peter Lavien, leaving Alexander and his brother without anything to support them. They were placed in the care of their cousin, Peter Lytton.

The two boys would be adopted by their cousin, then their uncle. Both men would die within short order, leaving the two boys without money or family.

James Hamilton Jr, Alexander's brother, would be apprenticed to a carpenter. Alexander, on the other hand, had already begun to work as a clerk for the two New York merchants, Beekman and Cruger. He would be taken in by Thomas and Ann Stevens, a wealthy and well respected merchant. Edward, the Stevens' oldest son, born a year before Hamilton, would become Alexander's close friend. They were also so close in appearance that many would assume they were in fact brothers. It would later be said that Thomas Stevens was Alexander's father. It would explain why Stevens took Hamilton in, and also give a name to one of the men Rachel had been accused of having an affair with.

Chapter Two: Hurricane

While working for the merchants, Hamilton gained immediate experience with the financial world, learning the costs of trading over long distance, how to convert money from one currency to another, and a number of other important skills that would serve him well.

For a time in 1771, due to Cruger's illness, he was actually left in charge of the trading house's branch on Nevis. He was not shy in giving advice and delivering tongue lashings to even experienced sea captains. Hamilton showed an aptitude for quick decisions and good judgement, though he would eventually have to return to his position as a clerk in 1772 when Cruger returned. Though the merchants traded mostly in food, they also did some trading in slaves.

An aspect of the large number of slaves on the islands was the constant problem of escapees, and the very real threat of a slave revolt. Free people were outnumbered by slaves by quite a wide margin. All the men on the island were required to be part of a militia, designed to help find escaped slaves and put a quick end to rebellion. Hamilton would undoubtedly been part of the militia, the first military experience he would have.

In 1770, the *Royal Danish American Gazette* began to publish. Hamilton, a self-taught young man, had found a place for his writing. He was soon submitting and publishing poems in its pages. His first two poems were both on the subject of love, but his later works were more religious. Hamilton would be influenced by Hugh Knox, a Presbyterian minister who arrived on the island. Knox would take Hamilton under his wing, providing more fodder for the younger man's insatiable mind, as well as doing his best to add some fun and lightness to Hamilton's, at that point, somewhat tragic life.

On August 21, 1772, a hurricane would tear through the Caribbean, destroying large swaths of property. Hamilton would write a letter describing it to his absent father, james Hamilton. Knox got a hold of the letter at some point, and as he sometimes served as editor or journalist for the *Gazette* he managed to get it published in the paper. The letter was well received by just about everyone who read it, being both an accurate description of facing the horror of a hurricane and poetic enough to be an affecting read. Even the governor of the island inquired after the letter's author. It so impressed the locals that a charity fund was created specifically to send Hamilton to North America to be educated. This is particularly amazing considering the devestation the island experienced in the wake of the hurricane.

Standard history has Hamilton sailing in October of 1772 for America. Evidence exists (particularly poems published in the *Gazette* that almost certainly were written by Hamilton) that he did not leave until 1773, however.

Another of Hamilton's cousins, Ann Venton, would primarily finance Hamilton's trip. She had moved to New York following the ending of her marriage and financial ruin, building a new life there. Hamilton believed he owed Ann such a debt that on the eve before his duel with Aaron Burr he mentioned Ann Lytton to his wife, saying that he still owed her a debt that he had not repaid.

Hamilton would leave his early life behind with his voyage to Boston. He would rarely speak of his childhood and life in the Caribbean, and never in specifics. He put all of his focus into creating a new life for himself in his new home.

Chapter Three: The Collegian

Hamilton received an allowance for his education from the islands. They would ship several kegs of sugar to New York, and Hamilton would pocket a percentage of their sale price to pay for his school and living.

With a talent for winning the confidence of important men that would stay with him throughout his life, Hamilton quickly made connections. The first was William Livingstone. A wealthy New Jersey man, Livingstone would later serve on the Continental Congress, as well as be New Jersey's first independent governor. Livingstone provided help, financial aid, and introductions to many influential people.

Princeton was founded by Presbyterians as a deliberate counter-balance to the pro-Anglican, monarchist tendencies in the colony. They would preach religious freedom, and according to the university president John Witherspoon the 'spirit of liberty' ran ' high and strong' among its students.

Hamilton applied to Princeton, asking for an accelerated course of study. This was not without precedent. The younger Aaron Burr had entered at 14 and graduated at 16 a few years earlier, and James Madison had completed his degree in just two years as well, working himself into a nervous exhaustion in the process. Witherspoon and Princeton's trustees would refuse his request, and instead he would attend King's College in New York. This was a center of pro-monarchist sentiment, which likely did more to embroil Hamilton in politics and the independence movement than if he had gone to the more radical, but isolated, Princeton.

Hamilton used his university literary club, a staple of college life at the time, to proof his anti-monarchist polemics. These were essays that Hamilton wrote criticizing England's policies. The tea tax, and the tea party that it motivated, occurred during Hamilton's college years, and he was quick to take the side of the revolutionaries. The British reaction, which mostly ignored or punished objectors, drove the various unhappy colonists together. The colonies had had very little common cause before the punishing of Boston. Now, they began to talk and plan together. Hamilton would give a fiery speech condemning the British Parliament's actions, making him something of a celebrity. He would take up the pen, writing political polemics and justifications for the rebels' cause. Hamilton developed his style at this time, that of charging into any disagreement as if it were a battle, and his opponent an adversary to be struck down, rather than someone to be convinced or charmed.

Chapter Four: The Pen And The Sword

With the revolution beginning in earnest, Hamilton joined the local militia, and devoted himself to studying military matters as well as his school work. Hamilton would study infantry tactics and maneuvers, and find a retired artilleryman to explain the basics of gunnery to him.

Hamilton would continue his writing, providing dispatches to the *Royal Danish American Gazette*, the newspaper on St Croix that was his first publishing forum. Though a rebel at heart, Hamilton would twice come to the defense of Loyalists who were the targets of mob violence. This would set a tone for his alter behavior.

Hamilton would be chosen as captain of an artillery company, trading on his self-taught knowledge. He was well regarded as a leader, seemingly having a natural talent for war and managing soldiers. At this point, Britain was beginning to take the colonial rebellion more seriously. A British warship would appear in New York harbor, and bombard the city, panicking the populace. Soon, the island of Manhattan would be invaded by an army of redcoats.

The British would chase the colonials off the island, Hamilton serving in the battle, but being forced to leave most of his cannon behind. He would see mixed success in the first days of the war, though that is true of the colonial cause in general. At any rate, his reputation as a soldier would only grow as time went on. Washington would lead his dwindling army south in further retreat, into New Jersey. Hamilton would follow. Throughout, he would continue his writing, and his reports of the battles would be published in the islands.

Chapter Five: The Little Lion

Hamilton would stay with the army during its retreat, earning a reputation as a steady commander that could manage his men well. Though ill with a fever, he would take part in the ambush on Trenton. He would also take part on the raid on Princeton, another colonial victory.

The pair of victories were a brief moment of light in the revolutionary cause, and bought the colonial army time to rest and resupply. Washington took Hamilton as an aide, a decision that would prove to be fateful for both men. In this capacity, Hamilton would meet many of the men that would play a large part in the political future of the United States. His appointment as Washington's aide would provide entree to the government that would later form.

Washington was not himself a great writer. Hamilton would be entrusted with a great deal of writing quickly becoming trusted to make decisions in Washington's place. This is also when Hamilton would meet the Marquis de Lafayette, the young French nobleman that would become a favorite of Washington's and a hero of the war. Along with John Lauren, the three men would be compared to the Three Musketeers in terms of closeness and willingness for adventure.

The colonies' fortunes in the war would change frequently. The colonial army remained small and ill supplied, while the British would repeatedly fail to take proper advantage of their victories. At one point, Washington dispatched Hamilton to order several companies of reinforcements to appear. This was an unusual appointment, particularly due to Hamilton's low rank and youth. That Hamilton succeeded shows his ability and diplomatic skills.

Hamilton would face many problems as Washington's aide. He was continually sick, including a malarial fever that would recur every summer. He would also make several enemies, notably the revolutionary hero Horatio Gates.

Chapter Six: A Frenzy of Valor
Hamilton, recovering from illness, would rejoin the Continental Army at Valley Forge. He would be horrified with the conditions here, where nearly a quarter of the army would die over the winter from lack of proper food and supplies. Hamilton would work with frenzy to find supplies for the army, which would also give him a chance to observe business in action, as well as the effect political policies can have on things like the availability of food. Inflation was a serious concern, as the Continental money was nearly valueless, leading farmers to take their food to the British to sell.

Hamilton would become close friends with Fredreich Wilhelm von Steuban. Claiming to be a baron (though he was not), von Steuban was a veteran soldier who came to the US specifically to help train the revolutionary soldiers. Speaking only a little English, von Steuban would often write and speak in French, relying on Hamilton or John Lauren to translate.

In 1778 the revolutionaries secured a treaty with France that included French military aid. A French army and navy would come to the colonies to fight on the revolutionaries' side. In response, the British put General Henry Clinton in charge. He marched on the Continental Army quickly, wishing to overwhelm them before the French could arrive. Washington wished to continue his policy of engaging the British in skirmishes and minor battles where their larger numbers would make less of a difference. The Virginian General Charles Lee believed the better policy was to wait for the French, with their better disciplined troops, to arrive. Though he was ordered to fight the British if an opportunity should arrive, he retreated. Hamilton, acting as a courier and scout, found the retreating Continental troops. He rallied them, ordering Lee to turn and fight.

Lee, after a court martial that resulted in a year long suspension from the army, would later take to criticizing Washington and his performance publicly, writing essays for publication and urging his supporters to do so also. This would eventually lead John Lauren to challenge the General to a duel. This was a common practice in the colonies at that time. Many men without real status or wealth found themselves in the middle class, or in the officer corps. Dueling was one of the few ways to protect their honor. Hamilton, for once, stayed out of the argument, perhaps because he had been called in to testify in the court martial. Both Lauren and Lee would survive, though Lee would retire from public life, back to Virginia.

Lauren and Hamilton would later work together on a project to recruit black slaves as soldiers with the promise of freedom after the war. Hamilton was skeptical of the then current notions of Africans' lack of intelligence and ability. However, their attempts to organize such a program failed.

Chapter Seven: The Lovesick Colonel

Hamilton began to look more seriously for a wife. He was not shy about flirting, and had been writing letters to several women over the years. He had met General Philip Schuyler in his time as Washington's aide, and most likely met Schuyler's children, and specifically his daughter Elizabeth. When General Schuyler came to Morristown, in the winter of 1779, he brought his family with him.

The winter was hard overall, with continuing problems with supplies and pay. Hamilton blamed many of these problems on the lack of centralized power and the weak Continental Congress. However, while the winter was difficult, it was a highly sociable one. The officers of the French army, now joined in the fight against the English, joined the families of many of the officers in Morristown. In 1779, Hamilton would be engaged to Elizabeth Schuyler, and then married to her in 1780.

Hamilton would also be one of the first witnesses of the most famous treacheries of the Revolutionary War, that of Benedict Arnold. Hamilton's arrival at West Point led Arnold to believe his treason had been discovered, and so he quickly fled to the British. Hamilton, who had no idea, would eventually uncover everything.

Despite the confidence Washington had in him and the access his position gave him, Hamilton wanted a command in combat. Tensions between him and Washington also began to rise. While the two had complementary personalities, they also could grate on each other. Finally, the two had an argument. Despite an attempt by Washington to make peace, their partnership ended.

Chapter Eight: Glory

Washington would continue as the General of the Continental Army for the rest of the war. Hamilton now had to find another job. He found a small house for himself and Eliza, and set about finding a military position for himself, enlisting the help of General Nathaniel Greene. He would succeed when given command of a light infantry company from New York.

While waiting for a command, Hamilton occupied himself in corresponding with his friends in government, and writing on finance and other issues. He believed a central bank was important to the country's long term success, as well as a structured debt to finance the war. Both of these would require a strong central government, something with more authority than the Continental Congress. Eventually, Congress would agree, and authority for direct decisions was given to several ministers, including one of finance. Hamilton's name was initially put forward, but he was passed over for Robert Morris, a wealthy merchant from Philadelphia.

A lucky confluence of events brought the French Navy within range to trap the British army under Cornwallis in the fort of Yorktwon. Washington marched his army, as did the French, to trap the British and complete the siege. Hamilton would lead one of the two companies that would take the final redoubts, forcing the British to surrender. The largest British army in the Americas had surrendered, and though both New York and large sections of the south were still under British control, the colonies had won their independence. Hamilton would make it through the war not just as a well connected, intelligent young man, but as a war hero as well.

Chapter Nine: Raging Billows

Hamilton moved to Albany with his family, joining his in-laws. He would be given a position as tax receiver for New York. The job was simple; the Continental Congress did not trust the states to collect the Continental taxes, and so they appointed receivers to collect the taxes for them. Hamilton took a small percentage as salary for his work.

He also opened a law firm, hoping to build a political career on a foundation of the law. However, he practiced only briefly before moving into a career as a Congressional representative.

At this point, Congress was essentially broke. They owe money to the army, sometimes as much as six years of backpay. The army was ready to mutiny, and only fast action kept it from doing so. Hamilton advised Washington to take his stand with the soldiers, and threaten military action if the money was not found to pay them. Washington instead walked a middle road, sending a delegation to Congress to advocate for the army, while convincing his men to wait for a peaceful solution. And one was eventually found, the Congress promising to pay a pension to the soldiers.

In 1783, a treaty was signed that officially ended hostilities with England. The British armies evacuated back to Europe and Canada, followed by many loyalists that had supported the King of England. Leaving the Congress, Hamilton avoided further public office, returning to the law.

Chapter Ten: A Grave, Silent, Strange Sort Of Animal

He would become a well known and successful lawyer. Practicing in New York, one of the busiest ports in the new United States, he spent a lot of time working on trade and insurance cases. Hamilton also devoted some portion of his time to pro bono cases, defending people who could not afford a good lawyer otherwise.

Aaron Burr would also become a lawyer in New York, though where Hamilton always sought to create new law, Burr depended on glibness and a convincing personality. They would work together several times, but oppose each other more frequently.

Hamilton would become famous for defending British Loyalists. The tide of opinion had turned violently against those who had remained loyal to the English crown. Laws were passed that stripped many of their property and made them essentially second class citizens. Like George Washington, Hamilton advocated for reconciliation, and as a result he would act as a lawyer for many loyalists seeking a return of money. It was during this time that Hamilton would evolve the concept of judicial review. This concept, that a judiciary could void an unconstitutional law, was a new one, and would be used later by Justice John Marshall to establish the power of the US Supreme Court, and help create the system that would become the checks and balance of the US government.

In 1784, Hamilton would help to found the Bank of New York, a government bank that would allow a greater range of trade, and return some stability to the chaotic finances of the colonies. Hamilton was on its board of directors, as well as having written most of its constitution, making him one of the more powerful men in the state in one stroke.

Chapter Eleven: Ghosts
Eliza and Alexander Hamilton would have eight children over twenty years of marriage, including adopting one orphan.

Hamilton was a strict abolitionist, and while he acted as intermediary, in his capacity as lawyer, for the sale of slaves for family and friends, he did not own any himself. Hamilton has a better record on this subject than just about every other Founding Father. He both continuously agitated for freedom for slaves, and never owned any himself, something that can be said for no other, not even John Adams. His contemporaries, even in the northern states (which had fewer slaves but still depended on black labor in many ways), were never as enthusiastic about abolitionism as he was.

Chapter Twelve: August And Respectable Assembly
Though Hamilton was initially opposed to returning to public service, he eventually was elected to the New York legislature. His particular enemy was New York Governor George Clinton. The two had been friendly during the war, when both were officers in the army. As time went on, their paths diverged, however. Clinton was strongly in favor of states rights, and conducted himself as the head of a small nation.

Hamilton was chosen to meet with delegates from the other states in Annapolis, Maryland in 1786. The point of this convention was to work out rules for negotiating inter-state trade agreements. The delegates quickly reached the conclusion that this was a complex question, and it would require not just new agreements, but a fundamental change to the Articles of the Confederation, the laws that governed the US before the Constitution. A new Constitutional Convention was called, and Hamilton was named as a delegate from New York.

It was a contentious meeting. The US was bankrupt, as were many of its citizens. The question of taxation (which had been a large part of what had driven the revolutionary movement) was still a central one, as it would fund the government and allow it to pay its debts. Many of the discussions and votes were conducted in closed meetings, and without records being kept. This allowed delegates to vote and discuss without the risk of recrimination. It would also allow rumors to fester, with an impact on Hamilton's later career.

In theory, the point was simply to amend the Articles of Confederation. It was quickly obvious that the Articles would be scrapped and a whole new document needed to be written, however. Two possible models were put forward. The New Jersey Plan would have each state receiving one vote in a theoretical legislature. The Virginia Plan would require that each state receive votes according to its population, as well as including the basic structure of the government that would be adopted with a bicameral legislature and three branches of government. At first, Hamilton uncharacteristically stayed silent.

When he broke his silence, he would propose a different plan, one that attempted to combine both democracy and monarchy. The chief executive and senate would serve for life, subject to recall. A house of representatives would sit for three years before new representatives were chosen. In this, it was based heavily on a British model of government. His proposal was not popular, for many reasons, and was largely ignored. Hamilton would be overruled by his fellow New York delegates, and would as a result drift back and forth between New York and the Convention. Shortly after his proposal, the Connecticut Compromise, that gives the US its present government, was reached. Though ambivalent about the plan, Hamilton would be part of the committee that would actually write the constitution, his eloquence once again taking center stage.

Chapter Thirteen: Publius

The proposed Constitution went far beyond the simple revisions of the Articles most people had expected, creating a much stronger central government. Two camps quickly organized themselves. Those in favor of the new Constitution were called federalists, and those against called anti-federalist.

Hamilton was seen as a champion of the federalists, and so he was attacked indirectly. Many essays were published by Governor Clinton's supporters, including some featuring a caricature called Tom Shit, an obvious reference to Hamilton. This would be the first time he would be 'accused' of being mixed race.

Seeing the need for a defense of the Constitution, Hamilton organized a series of essays, written by a few different people, but all published under the nom de plume of Publius. He would convince James Madison and John Jay to help him write these essays, though Hamilton would end up writing almost two thirds of the over eighty essays. They were initially published in newspapers, then collected in volumes.

The Constitution would only go into effect if nine states approved it. Several states approved it quickly. More wanted to impose conditions on their approval, the most popular being the inclusion of a bill of rights, amendments that listed individual rights and circumscribed governmental power. Hamilton was not in favor of the Bill of Rights, a rare failure of vision for him.

The *Federalist*, as the collected essays were called, have become a classic of governmental theory. In it, the authors lay out the justifications for the different parts of the proposed Constitution, elaborating on the situations that would require a strong central government. Hamilton himself brought his realistic, some might say pessimistic, view of humanity to the issue, making many arguments from the worst case rather than the best. A strong federal government would act as a check for the vices and corruption people were prone to.

The essays worked to a certain extent. They undoubtedly had an effect in some states. In Hamilton's home state of New York, however, the federalists had a harder time. Eventually, nine states voted to ratify, and the discussion in New York changed from whether to approve the constitution, to whether New York would be a part of the new country. The anti-federalists' cause lost some steam, and after an impassioned speech by Hamilton, the new Constitution was ratified in New York.

Chapter Fourteen: Putting The Machine In Motion
According to many, including Hamilton, George Washington was the only possible choice for the first president. He was the only one who could unite the new country, as well as keep it on an even keel and functioning correctly. Hamilton's nemesis, George Clinton, would also run. It was a strange mix of high minded political discourse and personal attacks that dominated the first election cycle of 1789.

Hamilton would be chosen as the first Secretary of the Treasury by Washington. He would take office and immediately leap into work. He was a natural and master administrator, and he probably did a great deal to save the US's credit, something that would be a strict necessity if the country was to survive. It required a deep understanding of the new Constitution as well, as he continuously wrestled with issues related to governmental problems. Washington would help to serve as a political buffer as Hamilton worked.

Chapter Fifteen: Villainous Business
Initially, the government was tiny With 39 employees, Hamilton had the largest department. The war department had only two people working in it beside Henry Knox, the new Secretary of War, when it was initially created.

William Duer was chosen as his under-secretary. Had invited him to write for the federalist, though he did not end up contributing. This would turn out be a poor choice. He would line his pockets with the inside knowledge his office gave him, and would babble to his friends about issues that required strict secrecy.

Hamilton set strict standards, divesting himself of any assets or entanglements that might have created a conflict. It is unfortunate that Duer's actions led to accusations of corruption that would follow Hamilton for the rest of his life.

Government debt became a hot button issue. Hamilton would frame the discussion to produce the result he wanted, and which would set a precedent for security and debt trading that continues to this day. He would, in the process, create the method for funding debt that the government, with some changes, still uses.

Chapter Sixteen: Doctor Pangloss

Thomas Jefferson would return from his time as representative to France to take up his office of Secretary of State. Jefferson and Hamilton had much in common. They were two of the best writers in the country, and both had predominantly gained their positions through their skill with the quill. They were both abolitionists, though Jefferson kept a number of slaves. And, indeed, the ways they were different proved to be more important.

Jefferson was a southern American aristocrat, having inherited a fortune. He was also very much against a strong central government. They would butt heads many times over the years, becoming the two bitterest rivals in early US political history.

There were two main issues on Hamilton's mind. The first was the federal assumption of the states' war debt. This would take the burden of paying the debt off the states, but it would strengthen the federal government's position, as well as giving the government an excuse to impose taxes.

The second issue was the new nation's capital. Hamilton wanted the temporary site to be New York, and the permanent site to be a northern city, such as Trenton. He negotiated, trying to gain both. However, the congress initially voted down his plan for assuming the debt. In exchange for giving up his ambitions for New York, however, a plan for passing a bill to assume the debt was made.

Chapter Seventeen: The First Town in America

Hamilton was a devoted family man, caring for his children and doing his best to be both encouraging and accepting of them. He seemed to have been very enthusiastic about education in general, tutoring his children, and becoming a trustee of a new school that would be named for him later.

He busied himself moving his department, with the rest of the government, to Philadelphia, something he did with the organization and aptitude with which he did everything. He also constructed the Customs Service and the Coast Guard. At this point, the federal government depended entirely on taxes for revenue, so a tight net on the coast was necessary, especially as, before and during the Revolution, smuggling and been a popular and patriotic activity.

The other major tax he advocated was an excise tax on liquor. This was extremely unpopular, but it was a better option than adding a tax to some other commodity. Hamilton did his best to make his collections with a light touch. Objections were very loud and passionate, however, and they would eventually lead to violence.

Chapter Eighteen: Of Avarice and Enterprise

The next legislative hurdle Hamilton would attempt to leap would be the creation of a national bank. He had already created s state bank in New York, and he would examine closely the history of banking, and the charter of the Bank of England. In this he would face the opposition of his one time political ally, James Madison, as well as Thomas Jefferson. They both felt that a central bank would favor the northern mercantile states to the detriment of the southern agrarian economies. Both these men also worried about governmental overreach, wanting to keep the government small.

The legislature passed the bill to create the bank easily, resulting in Jefferson trying to convince Washington to veto (the first veto in US history) the banking bill. Washington solicited opinions from his cabinet. Jefferson wrote an articulate paper against the bank, but Hamilton wrote a compelling, complete justification for a central bank, refining and explaining the doctrine of implied powers. Washington would sign the bill.

The bank would be funded through selling shares, publicly. A run on shares started, with by far most of the shares ending up in northern hands. This increased Jefferson and Madison's fears of a mercantile oligarchy taking power. Of more immediate concern to Hamilton was the fact that a run on bank stock was a boom that could quickly lead to a crash. Hamilton took several backroom steps to correct the problem, setting a precedent for similar arrangements in the future. However, he again left himself open to accusations of corruption and insider trading.

Hamilton also created the US mint and US coinage, including many aspects we would recognize such as pictures of presidents on coins and both copper and silver coinage.

Chapter Nineteen: City of the Future

In 1791, Hamilton began an affair with Maria Reynolds, a married woman. Her husband, James Reynolds, was a financial speculator and shady character. It is likely that he sent his wife to Hamilton, who had had several other affairs at this point and had a reputation for being a ladies man, with the specific intention of gaining power over the Treasury Secretary, with the hopes of blackmailing him, either for money or information. As soon as the scheme became apparent, Hamilton paid the Reynolds a large sum of money. Somewhat amazingly, Hamilton continued to see Maria even after this pay-off.

Hamilton was, at this point, working hard to encourage the industry of the US. He would seek out men who had worked in British factories, which kept many of their methods secret, in an early form of industrial espionage. He also helped to found the town of Paterson, New Jersey, with the specific intent that factory be built there. In a report to Congress, he laid out an economic plan for building the industrial capacity of the US. However, it addressed few of the practical urgent matters that required attention at that time, and was largely ignored.

Soon after Hamilton's friend and former under-secretary William Duer, ran into difficulties. Duer had a habit of using his position in government and as Hamilton's friend to speculate on the financial markets. Finally, the edifice of dependent contracts and borrowed money Duer had constructed fell apart. Duer begged Hamilton for help, particularly legal protection. Hamilton felt to help Duer would to weaken his position, his office's position, and the financial market he was laboring to build. Duer would go to prison, and die there, though the two would remain friends and Duer did not blame Hamilton.

Chapter Twenty: Corrupt Squadrons

The divide between Hamilton's mercantile goals and Jefferson and Madison's more libertarian ideals began to take on a more formal aspect. The first two political parties of the new country were forming. Hamilton's Federalists were in favor of a strong central government, and favored industrialization. Madison and Jefferson's Democratic-Republicans wanted more states' rights and a focus on agriculture. The Federalists also tended to favor closer a relationship with Britain, while the Democratic-Republicans preferred France.

Political parties were not part of the original design for the US's political system. Politicians would deny membership, seeing them as a liability rather than an advantage. Newspapers at the time were closer to opinion journals, and politicians on both sides began trading barbs in their pages. Jefferson, in particular, attacked Hamilton personally. He also warned Washington that Hamilton's Treasury Dept. was in danger of swallowing the government. Madison, meanwhile, was a master legislature and was organizing an attack on Hamilton from that quarter.

Jefferson did his best to convince Washington that Hamilton was at the head of 'a corrupt squadron' of voters in Congress, voting as Hamilton directed them. Hamilton retaliated against Jefferson in newspapers. Washington would attempt to negotiate peace, but would be unsuccessful.

Chapter Twenty-One: Exposure

James Reynolds continued to make demands for money into 1792, while Hamilton continued to see his wife. This continued until Hamilton began to fear his affair would injure his political position.

Reynolds was close friends with Jacob Clingman who had been secretary for a congressman. When they were arrested for defrauding the government, Clingman went to his former employer with hints he had information that might be interesting. Several of Jefferson's allies, including James Munroe, investigated the accusation that Hamilton had used his connection with Reynolds to speculate and use insider information to make a fortune.

Instead, Hamilton admitted the whole sordid affair. He showed all the documents he had relating to the matter, proving he was a victim of blackmail and not a speculator. The investigators pledged to keep the information to themselves. However, several indiscretions led to Jefferson learning of everything. Hamilton would continue with the knowledge that his bitterest rival now knew enough to ruin him.

Chapter Twenty-Two: Stabbed in the Dark

A presidential election was set for 1792. Washington was reluctant to stand for the office again. However, one of the few things both Jefferson and Hamilton agreed on was the necessity of his remaining in office. The northern and southern states were still at odds, and the new political parties still savaging each other in Congress and in the papers. Washington could keep the country united.

John Adams stood for vice president, against Hamilton' old enemy George Clinton. Aaron Burr also briefly ran for the office. However, he was forced to throw his support behind Clinton. For political reasons, Hamilton opposed Burr in his bid for the vice presidency. This would not be the last time Hamilton would keep Burr from achieving political office. In any event, Adams was once again chosen as vice president.

Jefferson and the Democratic-Republicans once again began searching for material to use against Hamilton. They came after him in Congress, requiring him to produce huge, detailed reports in a short amount of time. They found disgruntled former employees to accuse him of corruption. In every case, he proved his innocence and industry. If anything, however, this made his enemies fear him even more.

Chapter Twenty-Three: Citizen Genet

The issue of the French Revolution had become central to American politics. The Democratic-Republicans, following Jefferson's lead, tended to characterize it as a successor to the American Revolution, and the French as simply seeking the same sort of freedoms the Americans now had. Jefferson and his followers discounted reports of beheadings and the madness of the mob as exaggerations.

Hamilton and the Federalists were more inclined to be friendly to Britain, as the two countries still were linked through their economies. Hamilton feared that the US would be drawn into battles between European powers, and was most concerned with keeping the US neutral. This was made more difficult when, in 1793, Citizen Edmond Charles Genet arrived in the US as France's Ambassador. Republican France would soon after declare war on England, as well as several other countries. Genet agitated for help for France, as well as seeking to outfit French privateers in American ports with American sailors. He also had a plan of attacking French colonies in the new world using a mercenary army recruited in the US.

Washington declared neutrality in the European war, one which would drag on for twenty years. Hamilton sought Genet's recall to France, until the Terror began, and purges of moderate politicians began. Fearing for his life if he should return to France, Genet was granted asylum, and became a US citizen.

Chapter Twenty-Four: A Disagreeable Trade

Fever and sickness would come to the US. Many in the Treasury department, and the government as a whole, would become ill. President Washington and his cabinet would eventually move out of Philadelphia until the sickness passed.

Hamilton and Eliza would both become sick. They would be cared for by Edward Stevens, Hamilton's foster brother and close friend from childhood, with treatments then current in the Caribbean where Stevens had been a practicing doctor. This included dosing with quinan and teas meant to calm the stomach and reduce fevers

Meanwhile, the constant accusations of corruption were exhausting Hamilton. He would withstand every accusation and investigation, actually requesting one investigation be given more time to prove his innocence. He would eventually be decisively cleared of all wrong-doing. However, his name would forever be linked with accusations of corruption. Washington, perhaps exhausted by the partisan problems, would distance himself from Hamilton, though he did come to his defense in Congress. Thomas Jefferson would resign from his post as Secretary of State on December 31st, 1793. This might have initially been a relief to Hamilton, though events would prove that he could not relax quite yet.

Chapter Twenty-Five: Seas Of Blood

If the Democratic-Republicans' support of the French Revolution was complicated by the violence of the Terror, the Federalists fondness for the British faced another hurdle. The British had decided they had the right to stop and seize neutral ships entering French ports, something that had been until then considered illegal. They would seize over 250 ships, as well as dragging sailors off American ships, claiming they were British deserters. There may have been some truth to this; the US was a popular place for unhappy British soldiers to jump ship. However, they seized hundreds of sailors. It is unlikely they were all in fact British deserters. These same problems would lead to the war of 1812 in another few years.

Hamilton was put forward as a special envoy to the British to negotiate a resolution to these problems before a new war broke out. However, he proved to be too controversial a candidate. Supreme Court Chief Justice John Jay was chosen instead. At the same time, Washington was doing his best to remain neutral, denying American ports to French privateers while still taking a strong stance against Britain.

Chapter Twenty-Six: The Wicked Insurgents Of The West

The controversial excise tax the government had assessed at Hamilton's urging remained a contentious topic. In 1792, the customs agents and sheriff in charge of collecting these taxes in western Pennsylvania were menaced, and held captive. Eventually they would flee, afraid for their lives. The US would face its first real internal challenge, the Whiskey Rebellion.

Hamilton's strategy was to overwhelm the rebellious farmers with a show of force. He hoped to intimidate them into peace before any real violence could break out. Militias were raised in the states surrounding Pennsylvania and an army (larger than most of those that the US fielded in the revolution) marched into the rebellious areas. Hamilton, covering for Secretary of War Henry Knox as he took a brief leave, commanded the army. The rebellion was ended with no real violence or bloodshed.

Faced with new accusations (that he led the army in some aristocratic bid, among others), exhausted him. He would eventually resign as Secretary of the Treasury in January of 1795. Before his resignation, however, he would offer a plan to finance and pay off the country's debt completely. This was adopted shortly after he left the government, and would go on to do exactly as Hamilton planned, making the US's credit equal of any European nation.

Chapter Twenty-Seven: Sugar Plums and Toys

In England, John Jay had negotiated a treaty with the British. This would turn out to be one of the hot button issues of the time. Popular feeling was, to be kind, still divided when it came to England. This was aggravated by the terms of the treaty itself, which were nowhere close to what the Americans had hoped. Washington kept the terms secret, and rushed its passage through the Senate. They passed it, with reservations.

The terms of the treaty were leaked, leading to demonstrations throughout the country against it. Hamilton assembled a counter-demonstration in New York, though he would not get a chance to speak. As he began, several people threw stones at him, one hitting him on the forehead. He would also challenge two opponents to duels, though both would eventually back down.

Hamilton was essentially broke at this point, his salary as Treasury Secretary not enough to support his growing family. However, he would turn down opportunities for land speculation and other get-rich-quick schemes in favor of returning to his law practice.

Jefferson and his political party would do their best to oppose the treaty. The unspoken rule that Washington would not be attacked was ignored, and he would be widely criticised. As Madison and Jefferson began to criticize Washington, the President began to favor Hamilton even more heavily. Hamilton would advise him on several issues, though he was no longer in government.

Chapter Twenty-Eight: Spare Cassius

Hamilton had begun to make three or four times as a lawyer as he had as a member of government. His personal fortunes were on the rebound, however, even while presenting cases in court he was still a political animal. He presided as one of the leaders of the Federalist party, it's chief tactician and theorist. In addition, he would often help Washington and his cabinet with advice and policy decisions. When Washington determined not to run for a third term (a tradition that was to stand until FDR, after whom it would be made into law), it was with Hamilton that he wrote his farewell address.

The following presidential race was close. Adams ran as the Federalist candidate, though Hamilton in truth preferred another, a man named Pickney, and worked quietly to promote him over Adams. Jefferson ran for the Democratic-Republicans, with Aaron Burr running for their vice-presidential seat.

Hamilton would write a number of essays and articles, culminating in a final one that would closely examine Jefferson, making him appear a poor choice compared to Adams. Among other things, there is evidence that Hamilton knew Jefferson was having an affair with a female slave, Sally Hemmings, that Hamilton hinted at in the essay.

Adams would be elected president, with Jefferson being chosen as his vice president. Pinckney would finish third, with Burr trailing a distant fourth. Adams resented Hamilton's backroom maneuvering against him, something that would come back to haunt Hamilton.

Chapter Twenty-Nine: The Man In The Glass Bubble
Adams was a problematic politician and a difficult president. He was a vain man, and had a tendency to burst out in fits of temper. He would write irritated, ill considered criticisms of even his friends, and others were frequently casually dismissed. Hamilton and Adams shared many political views. However, their personalities were too much at odds. Adams disliked Hamilton's ambition, and often ignored him. Hamilton wished to still be of use at the center of government.

Adams would frequently be absent from Washington D.C., visiting his home in Massachusetts. He had a very different style of governing than President Washington had used, leading to some resentment among his cabinet.

Chapter Thirty: Flying Too Near The Sun
Hamilton's Scottish relatives made contact. This was gratifying to Hamilton, even though what they required was a job for Hamilton's estranged Scottish cousin, newly arrived in the US. Similarly, but more welcome, Eliza Hamilton's sister Angelica Church and her husband, John Church, moved to the United States. John had been a member of British Parliament, but on losing his seat he decided to bring his wife back to her family.

The heaviest personal attacks on Hamilton would begin, dredging up the issue of Maria Reynolds and Hamilton's infidelity. Now, however, it was suggested that the whole affair had been merely a cover for illicit financial transactions. Papers that Hamilton had entrusted to certain men were used as proof of the affair. The accusations of corruption had no evidence to support them. Hamilton leaped to his own defence, publishing a pamphlet admitting the affair but denying any financial wrongdoing.

At the same time, he sought to find the person responsible for supplying evidence of the affair to his accusers. In this, he blamed James Munroe, who indeed had passed the papers to another man to copy, who had then used information to slander Hamilton. Munroe and Hamilton nearly fought a duel over the issue, but peace was restored by Aaron Burr. Burr was tapped to act as a go between, and by advising caution and cunning delays, managed to put the issue off until both men settled down.

Chapter Thirty-One: An Instrument Of Hell

Relations between the US and France soured after the Jay treaty was adopted. France began seizing US ships heading to Britain, mirroring British behavior. American Democratic-Republicans found themselves supporting a country that might soon be at war with the US.

American delegates were sent to France to negotiate a peace, but without initial success. The matter of a standing army had become central to the government. Most of the Founding Fathers were against maintaining a standing army, saying that they are chiefly used to trample the liberties of the people. However, with war on the horizon it was appearing necessary to create both a standing army and navy.

Washington was chosen to lead the army, and he chose Hamilton as his second in command. This did not please many, and in fact the wrangling over who would be an officer and commander in the new army caused many rifts between the two political parties, and between Hamilton and Adams.

Eventually, peace would be negotiated, and the new army would not be needed. But the politicking that had been necessary to create it would create ripples that would have consequences for many years.

Chapter Thirty-Two: Reign of Witches

The Federalists had gained control of the government. They quickly passed a series of laws known as the Alien and Sedition Acts. These gave wide powers to the president and government to deport immigrants as well as prosecute libel, slander, and sedition (which is writing and publishing things that are critical of the government).

The Democratic-Republicans saw these laws as over-reaching, and knew the Federalists had bit off more than they could chew. Jefferson and Madison began secretly writing acts to be passed in state legislatures, calling the new laws unconstitutional, which they undoubtedly were. Hamilton, on the other hand, used the laws to prosecute many of the newspapers that had been heaping accusations on him.

A minor rebellion began, once again in Pennsylvania, motivated by new taxes and rumors. Hamilton once more marched with the new army, overwhelming the rebels with force. It was quickly put down, but doubts were beginning to circulate about the wisdom of dealing with such issues in that way.

Chapter Thirty-Three: Works Godly And Ungodly

Hamilton was occupied with his family, and also with the New York Manumission Society, a group that advocated the end of slavery. In 1798, the society managed to bring an end to slavery in New York and New Jersey, getting the Legislature to pass a law forbidding it in those states.

Aaron Burr, meanwhile, was plotting to get back into the good graces of the Democratic-Republicans. Yellow fever had broken out in New York, the result of unclean water. A doctor proposed a plan to pump clean water from the nearby Bronx River to prevent further outbreaks. Burr seized upon this, outlining a private company that would raise the money and provide the water.

New York had only Federalist banks at that time, and Burr decided he could break that monopoly with a little chicanery. When it came time to pass the bill allowing the water company, named the Manhattan Company, he inserted an amendment at the last moment that would allow the company much wider powers. It passed without anyone the wiser. Burr quickly used this new freedom to make the Manhattan Company a bank. Instead of pumping clean water, it used the same contaminated water, and yellow fever broke out once more.

While a politically astute move, it did not play well with the electorate. Burr lost his seat in the New York legislature. He also fought a duel with Hamilton's brother in law, John Church, though neither was harmed.

Chapter Thirty-Four: In An Evil Hour
While most of the negotiators returned from France, President Adams was still attempting to craft a peaceful solution. Adams would clash with his own party, his own cabinet, and with Hamilton over how to handle France. The Federalists preferred a close relationship with Britain, and Hamilton was relying on the threat of France to motivate the raising of the standing army he was organizing. Adams would end up insulting most of the Federalists, Hamilton in particular, in the process of crafting a peaceful resolution to the conflict (called the Quasi War in historical texts).

Soon after, Washington would die. He and Hamilton had been close to the end. With his death, the one thing keeping the Federalist party together died as well. Hamilton would resign his military role, and would blame Adams for the collapse of his military hopes, as well as the factionalism in the Federalist party.

Chapter Thirty-Five: Gusts of Passion
Hamilton and Burr would work together, surprisingly, on a pro bono criminal defense case. Shortly thereafter, they would find themselves on opposites sides once more. The New York elections arrived, Burr using all of his political acumen to arrange a coalition of Democratic-Republicans (all enemies of Hamilton) to run against the Federalist slate Hamilton and his aides had created. Burr would shepherd his own candidates to a win, thus securing for himself the nomination as the Democratic-Republican Vice President.

Adams and Hamilton continued to snipe at each other. Adams would dismiss his cabinet, most of whom were friends of or sympathetic to Hamilton. With the death of Washington, Hamilton's entree to government was at its lowest ebb. Hamilton quietly supported another Federalist candidate, the same Charles Pinckney, over reelecting Adams, and he would tour the country raising support for him, while seemingly supporting Adam in his reelecton bid. Adams was not fooled.

Chapter Thirty-Six: In A Very Belligerent Humor

Adams was known for a sometimes uncontrolled temper, and for extended fits of anger. Never a great respecter of Hamilton, he would launch several attacks on him, in private and in the pages of newspapers. Hamilton began by asking privately for a retraction (with a hint of the threat of a duel in the message), and finished by publishing a long pamphlet criticizing Adams. Hamilton, as a gentlemen, felt compelled to sign his name to the document.

It was widely published, causing a rift in the Federalist party. A small group sided with Hamilton, but most stayed loyal to the sitting president. In 1801, Jefferson and Burr would win the presidency, though it is unlikely Adam's and Hamilton's fight affected the outcome. In the coming years, the rifts in the Federalist party would grow larger, and it would eventually cease to exist. While the part existed, however, it guided the country through its important early years, and set the tone for much of what would come after.

Chapter Thirty-Seven: Deadlock

A peace was concluded with France, justifying Adams' preference for diplomacy over armed conflict. It came as Jefferson took the presidency, however, with Aaron Burr elected vice president.

At the time, elections worked somewhat differently. Four candidates ran for the presidency. The one who received the most votes in the electoral college became president, and whoever received the second most votes became vice-president. Burr and Jefferson tied, initially, and so more ballots were necessary to break the deadlock. Hamilton threw his support behind Jefferson, as while he disagreed with Jefferson's principles, he suspected Burr lacked any principles at all.

Jefferson eventually made a backroom deal with the Federalists and Hamilton, and was elected President.

Chapter Thirty-Eight: A World Full Of Folly

Hamilton had lost most of his political power. Ironically, in becoming Vice President Burr also surrendered most of his political power. They tussled over the New York gubernatorial race, but its outcome was more likely determined by Jefferson's input than either Burr's or Hamilton's.

Eliza and their family moved to a farmhouse, with Hamilton focusing once more on his law practice and his family. Hamilton's fear that Jefferson's election would mean the end of strong federal government turned out to be foundless. Jefferson found the machinery of a strong government too useful to discard.

Life quieted, until Hamilton's oldest son, Philip, was involved in a duel. Philip would be killed, shot in the stomach. Another of Hamilton's children, Angelica, would suffer a breakdown and spend the rest of her life only occasionally lucid.

Chapter Thirty-Nine: Pamphlet Wars
Lamenting the loss of his political power, Hamilton once again picked up the pen. Each of the factions in Washington had their own newspaper. Hamilton started the *New York Evening Post*, now the longest continually running newspaper, and Burr and the Democratic-Republicans started their own paperl. They exchanged written attacks in what is called the Pamphlet Wars. Dueling was also increasingly popular, often as an extension of the personal attacks in the papers. Hamilton seemed conflicted on dueling, adhering to a gentlemanly code while acknowledging the violence of dueling.

Burr found himself with nowhere to turn for political clout but his one-time enemies, the Federalists. Some sided with him, though his influence was ultimately small. Burr, Hamilton, Jefferson, and others attacked each other in the press, in endless, pointless personal assaults.

Chapter Forty: The Price Of Truth
Hamilton mellowed the further removed from politics he was. He returned to practicing law, and writing about constitutional law and theory rather than delving into practical politics. He was drawn back into the political sphere when he defended a newspaper publisher that had been arrested for sedition, being critical of Jefferson. Hamilton would lose, but the arguments he evolved for the defense came to be adopted when it came to pass laws regarding questions of libel and slander.

In 1803, seeking a base of political power, Aaron Burr ran for New York governor. Hamilton's assessment of Burr's plan was that he would use this as the center of a new northern confederacy, and perhaps Burr's ultimate goal was to break the union, with himself in a position of power. Hamilton threw his support behind Burr's opponent once again.

The personal attacks continued, and though Burr maintained a public facade of indifference, privately he blamed Hamilton for the worst of the attacks. Burr believed he could win, however when the votes were counted he lost by a wide margin. Burr now blamed Hamilton not just for blocking his run for the Presidency, but now also the governorship of New York. More than that, he saw Hamilton as the author of a range of horrible personal attacks.

Chapter Forty-One: A Despicable Opinion
There is no doubt that Burr blamed Hamilton for many of the attacks. There may also have been a cold-blooded aspect to his challenging Hamilton to a duel. By defeating his opponent, Burr might have calculated that his political stock would rise again. Hamilton, in contrast, could not believe that Burr would actually shoot to kill, that being very rare in pistol duels. Hamilton himself planned to hold his fire, allow Burr to shoot, then call the matter ended. He would attend the duel because otherwise he would be dishonored and would likely no longer be able to serve in government, not because he believed in the practice.

Burr, however, was practicing shooting on a daily basis. Hamilton did very little to prepare for his death, keeping the matter to himself, and outlining a will to deal with his finances, primarily debt. In the spring of 1804, the two men would finally meet.

Chapter Forty-Two: Fatal Errand

Hamilton spent the days before the duel with his family, and working. Burr spent it mostly alone, worrying over money and creditors. Amazingly, Burr applied to Hamilton for financial assistance, and Hamilton polled his friends to raise a great deal of money to help Burr out of debt.

The two men rowed to an island, with the seconds and a doctor, for the duel. As planned, Hamilton wasted his shot, aiming away from Burr. Burr, in return, fired a deadly bullet into Hamilton's side. Hamilton immediately knew it was a fatal wound. He would be returned to his home, where he would slip in and out of consciousness. Eliza would learn of the duel and its outcome, and spend the next two days by her husband's side. His friends and family would visit him briefly, before he died in his sleep.

The city of New York paused in general mourning for the passing of Alexander Hamilton.

Chapter Forty-Three: The Melting Scene

New York stopped for Hamilton's funeral, all businesses closing. The citizens wore black armbands for a month, and both the courthouse and Bank were draped in black. Hamilton was eulogized by his friend Gouverneur Morris, who struggled to find words to describe Hamilton, so large a figure and containing so many contradictions.

Aaron Burr never showed real remorse for killing Hamilton, believing he had followed the forms of dueling and had done nothing wrong. Things he said later in life, however, tends to indicate he intended to kill Hamilton from the start. In any case, it was the end of his political career. He left New York, fleeing creditors and possible murder charges. He would travel in the south, where Hamilton was unpopular and his death greeted with some pleasure. He would return to preside over his final session of Congress as Vice President. Burr would go on to travel in Europe and the New World, occasionally spinning schemes to forge new kingdoms, in the west or in Mexico.

Burr would eventually return to New York where he would die alone, his family having passed years earlier. He would be tried for treason as a result of some of his schemes, be acquitted, and then fade into obscurity.

Epilogue: Eliza

Eliza would live until 1854, when she would die at the age of ninety-seven. She had struggled to raise her children on the modest income she badgered out of various government administrations. All of the Hamilton childrenwere successful, becoming lawyers, military men, and and politicians. She would always champion her husband's memory. Most of her time in later life was occupied with charitable pursuits, in particular working with orphans. She would eventually oversee the grand biography of Alexander Hamilton written by his son.

Biographies

Alexander Hamilton September 11, 1755 - January 31, 1795

Born in the Caribbean, illegitimate son of a minor Scottish nobleman, Hamilton had very modest beginnings. Most of his family would die or lose contact with him, effectively orphaning him. It was primarily through hard work and intelligence that Hamilton made his life as successful as it was.

Based on his writing, he became well known and popular enough that a fund was setup to send him to school. Enough money was collected for him to travel to New York, enter college there, and support himself until he graduated. Shortly after, he would become a lawyer. His legal career would last until his death, though he would often take years long breaks away from practicing law. During these times he would serve as a military officer, have a high place in government, and do a great deal to write the laws he would later interpret.

An intelligent, energetic man, Hamilton was not known for his diplomacy. His beliefs drove him fiercely, and often drove him into conflicts that he might have avoided through quieter words. However, he held his beliefs strongly, and would act always in accordance with his principles. He understood the far reaching consequences that the decisions he and his colleagues made could have, and he labored to ensure the best possible results. In creating and writing most of *The Federalist*, he crafted one of the most important justifications for strong central government. It is a work that is still read, studied, and admired today.

Though he was indiscreet in a number of ways, it is likely that many of the accusations of infidelity against him were untrue. The exception, of course, being the affair with Maria Reynolds, for which there is ample evidence and which Hamilton admitted. However, there was no evidence for any of the many accusations of corruption that started almost as soon as he entered government. He was investigated any number of times, and in all cases cleared of wrongdoing. It has been suggested that Hamilton was a monarchist, in favor of an aristocracy, and many other things that would seem to put him at odds with the American Revolution's focus on liberty and equality. However, many, if not most, of these accusations are the result of the vile personal attacks that were part of politics at that time. It is likely most were distortions of his true positions, if not entirely fabricated. Unfortunately, many of these accusations have come to color the public perception of him and his work.

In all things, he sought to serve the American people and the government. It was this last trait that may have, in some ways, led to his death. Though he had been growing less convinced of the merits of dueling, the political necessity of maintaining his reputation led him to fight Aaron Burr.

Alexander Hamilton left a mark on the US, creating many of the institutions that are still with us, part of our society and government, to this day.

Eliza Hamilton August 9, 1757 - November 9, 1854

Born into the wealthy and influential Schuyler family, Eliza was a pretty woman who was destined to become part of the American Colonies' upper crust. Her father, Philip Schuyler, was a wealthy merchant, and would later become a Revolutionary General and US statesman.

Eliza was actually barely literate, which is interesting considering her husband's profligate writing. She worked hard in many ways, however, keeping a household together despite the fact that the Hamiltons were frequently deep in debt, and also working for many charitable causes, particularly the care of orphans. She would give birth to all of Hamilton's eight children, and do the majority of the work raising them, as Hamilton was often absent.

After Alexander Hamilton's death, Eliza would remain unmarried, loyal to the man she still loved. It was at her urging that Hamilton's son, John Hamilton, would complete a multi-volume biography of his father.

Eventually, she would move to Washington D.C., where she would pass away at the age of ninety-seven.

George Washington February 22, 1732 - February 11, 1731

Washington's family was part of the minor English gentry, having moved to the American Colonies. Washington's father would buy and inherit several properties. George would inherit two, Ferry Farm, and upon the death of his brother Lawrence, Mount Vernon.

Washington never received a higher education, which is likely why he leaned on Hamilton and the other college graduates in his military and later cabinet for many opinions and to help in his writing. Washington himself would receive an early education in surveying, which would be his first career. He would do his best, through tutoring and reading, to make up his lack of education.

Washington sought advancement through a military career, joining the Virginia Militia. He was generally looked down on by the British regulars, though a few noticed his intelligence and ability. He was sent in 1753 to meet with several Native American leaders to secure their aid in the case of a war with France. He did this, then proceeded on the second part of his task: to protect British colonists in the Ohio Country, an area west of the Appalachian mountains and south of Lake Erie. French soldiers had already driven out the colonists and started construction of a fort, however. Washington ambushed some of these soldiers, winning a minor victory.

He would be part of the Braddock disaster, when a British force led by General Braddock was ambushed and destroyed by the French and their Native American allies. Though he worked to hard to save many soldiers, this was a failure that would follow him all his life.

Washington would retire to Mount Vernon, returning to public life when elected to the Continental Congress. Shortly thereafter he would be chosen as the General of the Continental Army. He would lead the revolutionary forces in the war until their final victory at Yorktown. Eventually, he would be elected the first president.

Though he did his best to stay neutral in the partisan politics of the time, he would lean heavily on Hamilton for advice, and tend to favor the federalist position of a strong central government. He would retire after two terms as president, having guided the new country through some of its most turbulent and difficult times.

He would die on Mount Vernon of a fever, mourned by the whole nation.

John Adams October 30, 1735 - July 4, 1826

Born as a member of a farming family in Massachusetts, Adams was keenly aware of his family's history. They had first come to the New World in the 17th century, as puritans fleeing religious persecution. Adams was known as a pugnacious man, not terribly diplomatic, but intelligent enough to often be infuriatingly correct.

He would enter Harvard college at the age of 16, and though his father wished him to become a minister, he followed a different path. After teaching school briefly, he became a lawyer, a role that would put him in the front lines of Massachusetts' disagreements with the British government. Though Adams would become a vocal advocate for independence, he would defend the British in the trial that would result from the Boston Massacre.

Adams would be elected to the Continental Congress, and would be instrumental in crafting the movement for independence, and eventually take part in the writing of the Declaration. He would go on to serve as a politician for the remainder of his life, only occasionally returning to the law. He would become an ambassador to Great Britain, to France, as well as being the first Vice President and the second President of the US.

Adams was not a universally popular man, and what may have been mistaken for fiery passion during the Revolution would turn out to be undiscriminating and poorly controlled temper. He would make himself unpopular through temper tantrums and poorly considered words.

After his defeat in the presidential election of 1801, he would retire from public life, beginning an autobiography he would never finish. Though he would be a fierce political opponent of Jefferson, the two would eventually make peace before dying on the same day.

Aaron Burr February 6, 1756 - September 14, 1836
Burr is typical of many of the characters that lurk around the edges of the Revolution. These men acted, not out of a sense of principle, but rather because they sensed an opportunity for advancement. In many ways Burr's and Hamilton's careers paralleled each other. Burr was

given entrance to Princeton and allowed to work and graduate early, where Hamilton was refused the same option.

Both men served on Washington's staff during the war. Hamilton had to be drafted into the position, and would continually seek a combat role. Burr would do his best to remain in the orbit of powerful men, leaving Washington's staff only to join another. After the war, the two men would practice law, sometimes together but frequently opposing one and other. Hamilton's career was based on novel interpretations of law and precedence. Burr would more often rely on glibness and a charming personality.

Hamilton was staunchly in favor of a strong federal government. Burr would send his political career moving back and forth between the Federalist and Democratic-Republican parties, choosing whichever was more likely to lead to his advancement. He would work in one capacity in government or another, putting himself forward as candidate for political office several times. That he would hold the position of Vice President is a testament to his intelligence and skill. However, that was as far as he would rise, however, and he would soon find his political capital entirely spent, losing the race for New York governor quite badly. He would blame Hamilton unfairly for this loss.

After Hamilton's death, he would travel in Europe and the US. His only family, his daughter, her husband, and their son, all passed away before Burr, leaving him essentially alone.

He would constantly put forward plans to lead expeditions to South America and Mexico to oust the Spanish, always with an eye to putting himself at the top of the heap. Eventually, he would put together a conspiracy to carve out a part of the western United States as a separate nation. It is unlikely any of the conspirators, with the exception of Burr, ever took the scheme seriously. The conspiracy would collapse, and Burr would be arrested for treason. He would be acquitted of all charges, though this was the final step to his complete disgrace.

Burr retired to New York, and led a very quiet, lonely life before dying in 1836

Thomas Jefferson April 13, 1743 - July 4, 1826
Jefferson was born in Virginia. His father, Peter, was a farmer and surveyor, two professions Jefferson would also take up later in his life. Peter Jefferson passed away when Thomas was just 14 years old, leaving his two sons a large amount of land. Thomas Jefferson would inherit 5,000 acres as well as the site where he would later design and build what would be his home for the rest of his life, Monticello.

Jefferson entered the College of William and Mary at the age of 16, which was the norm for that time. Jefferson also spent a great deal of his own time reading and studying, and would assemble a library of over 6,000 volumes through his life.

In addition to being a farmer and surveyor, Jefferson would be admitted to the Virginia bar and practice as a lawyer, as well as representing Albemarle County in Virginia's House of

Burgesses, the colony's legislative body. Though Jefferson owned slaves himself, he would take a variety of cases involving slaves seeking freedom. In this capacity, he would begin to articulate several of the arguments that would shape his thinking and policies in the Continental Congress and beyond.

Marrying Martha Wayles Skelton in 1772, he soon had a family of his own. Martha would give birth to six children, though only two would live through childhood, infant mortality being a serious problem at that time. Jefferson would later be said to be happiest when with Martha and his family at Monticello.

Beginning in 1775, Jefferson would be named as one of Virginia's representatives to the Second Continental Congress. Jefferson would become good friends with John Adams. This most likely led to him being named to the Committee of Five, the members of the Continental Congress charged with writing the Declaration of Independence. Known as a talented and articulate writer, Jefferson would shoulder the bulk of the writing, though he did receive input from other members of the Committee, in particular John Adams and Benjamin Franklin. Notably, Jefferson's original draft contained several passages that were later removed, including one sharply critical of slavery.

Jefferson would go on to serve as Virginia's Governor, as well returning to the House of Burgesses and the US Congress. Following the death of his wife Martha, he would travel to Europe to serve as the United States Minister to France. It was here that he would first face the problem of the Barbary Corsairs.

Jefferson would serve as the First Secretary of State, the second Vice President, and the third President. He would oversee negotiations that would lead to the Louisiana Purchase, and dispatch Lewis and Clark on their famous exploration, in addition to making many other decisions and evolving a number of policies that would shape the course of the United States' growth. It would be under his guidance that the new nation would begin to face the issue of piracy in the Mediterranean, though the conflict would reach its ultimate resolution under his successor, James Madison.

Generally considered one of the finest minds the US has ever produced, Thomas Jefferson wrote on a broad range of topics, from diplomacy and law to mathematics. His religious beliefs were remarkably modern for his time, and included some sharp criticism of several aspects of Christianity.

Though he frequently agitated against the practice of slavery, he himself owned slaves and partook of many of the practices he criticised, including separating members of families by selling them away to other owners. In 1998, a DNA test confirmed that Jefferson fathered at least one child with a slave named Sally Hemmings. Hemmings gave birth to six children, four of whom survived to adulthood, and all of whom were eventually freed. Many historians believe these were all Jefferson's children. Sally Hemmings, however, remained a slave until

Jefferson's death, when she was also finally freed. Hemmings was herself a half sister of Jefferson's wife, Martha Wayles Skelton, proving that such liaisons were not entirely unusual.

Jefferson has been characterized as a polymath, advocate of freedom, and staunch pacifist. In recent years, however, he has come under renewed scrutiny, and some aspects of his life that are less complimentary have come to light. He took a large part in the first removal from traditional lands and resettlement of Native Americans, believing they should abandon their traditional culture and beliefs in preference for European culture. His treatment of his slaves is also seen as being at odds with his stated belief in freedom for all.

Jefferson was a staunch anti-federalist, and opposed the expansion of Federal powers. He did take part in founding the first Republican party, also called the Democratic-Republican party. However, this is not the same as the modern conservative party, which was founded in the 1850's. At this point, no politician wanted to be connected to a political party, as they were considered remnants of the British system of government. However, partisan politics became a huge aspect of American government as well.

The few years when the Federalist party and Democratic-Republican parties, led by Hamilton and Jefferson respectively, were competing for government seats is perhaps one of the most acrimonious eras of US politics. It's easy to understand why. The men involved had only recently fought what many thought was a hopeless war to create their own country. Having done that, they then wrangled with creating a new government, and all the complex questions that such a task would prompt. It is hard to balk at anything when you genuinely believe, as many politicians at that time did, that your opponent's actions could genuinely lead to anarchy or tyranny. As a result, personal assaults, both in print and in person, were not unusual. Dueling, fights, and other physical altercations were also a part of the US political scene.

Jefferson remains a complex figure, a man who had a large part in forming the United States and laying down its foundational principles, while in many cases acting against those principles.

Made in the USA
Middletown, DE
20 April 2018